DATE	PLACE	TIME	WEATHER		
HOME	LEAGUE	SEASON	OPPONENT		

MW01052659

SINGLES | RECORDS | | MATCH SCORES

No	HOME				SET 2	SET 3	WINNER
1							
2							
3							
4							
5							
6							

TENNIS
TENNIS SCORE RECORD

DOUBLES | RECORDS | | MATCH SCORES

No	HOME	H	O	OPPONENT	SET 1	SET 2	SET 3	WINNER
1								
2								
3								

	TOTALS				

TENNIS SCORE SHEET

DATE	PLACE	TIME	WEATHER	COURT CONDITIONS	
HOME	LEAGUE	SEASON	OPPONENT	LEAGUE	SEASON

SINGLES

No	HOME	RECORDS H	RECORDS O	OPPONENT	SET 1	SET 2	SET 3	WINNER
1	Ollie	O		Tyler	3			
2	Alexander	1		George	2			
3								
4								
5								
6								

DOUBLES

No	HOME	RECORDS H	RECORDS O	OPPONENT	SET 1	SET 2	SET 3	WINNER
1								
2								
3								

TOTALS

TENNIS SCORE SHEET

DATE	PLACE	TIME	WEATHER	COURT CONDITIONS	
HOME	LEAGUE	SEASON	OPPONENT	LEAGUE	SEASON

SINGLES

No	HOME	RECORDS H	RECORDS O	OPPONENT	SET 1	SET 2	SET 3	WINNER
1								
2								
3								
4								
5								
6								

MATCH SCORES

DOUBLES

No	HOME	RECORDS H	RECORDS O	OPPONENT	SET 1	SET 2	SET 3	WINNER
1								
2								
3								

MATCH SCORES

	TOTALS				

TENNIS SCORE SHEET

DATE	PLACE	TIME	WEATHER	COURT CONDITIONS	
HOME	LEAGUE	SEASON	OPPONENT	LEAGUE	SEASON

SINGLES		RECORDS			MATCH SCORES			
No	HOME	H	O	OPPONENT	SET 1	SET 2	SET 3	WINNER
1								
2								
3								
4								
5								
6								

DOUBLES		RECORDS			MATCH SCORES			
No	HOME	H	O	OPPONENT	SET 1	SET 2	SET 3	WINNER
1								
2								
3								
		TOTALS						

TENNIS SCORE SHEET

DATE	PLACE	TIME	WEATHER	COURT CONDITIONS	
HOME	LEAGUE	SEASON	OPPONENT	LEAGUE	SEASON

SINGLES

No	HOME	RECORDS H	RECORDS O	OPPONENT	SET 1	SET 2	SET 3	WINNER
					MATCH SCORES			
1								
2								
3								
4								
5								
6								

DOUBLES

No	HOME	RECORDS H	RECORDS O	OPPONENT	SET 1	SET 2	SET 3	WINNER
					MATCH SCORES			
1								
2								
3								

	TOTALS		

TENNIS SCORE SHEET

DATE	PLACE	TIME	WEATHER	COURT CONDITIONS	
HOME	LEAGUE	SEASON	OPPONENT	LEAGUE	SEASON

SINGLES		RECORDS			MATCH SCORES			
No	HOME	H	O	OPPONENT	SET 1	SET 2	SET 3	WINNER
1								
2								
3								
4								
5								
6								

DOUBLES		RECORDS			MATCH SCORES			
No	HOME	H	O	OPPONENT	SET 1	SET 2	SET 3	WINNER
1								
2								
3								

	TOTALS			

TENNIS SCORE SHEET

DATE	PLACE	TIME	WEATHER	COURT CONDITIONS	
HOME	LEAGUE	SEASON	OPPONENT	LEAGUE	SEASON

SINGLES

No	HOME	RECORDS H	RECORDS O	OPPONENT	SET 1	SET 2	SET 3	WINNER
1								
2								
3								
4								
5								
6								

MATCH SCORES

DOUBLES

No	HOME	RECORDS H	RECORDS O	OPPONENT	SET 1	SET 2	SET 3	WINNER
1								
2								
3								

MATCH SCORES

	TOTALS				

TENNIS SCORE SHEET

DATE	PLACE	TIME	WEATHER	COURT CONDITIONS	
HOME	LEAGUE	SEASON	OPPONENT	LEAGUE	SEASON

SINGLES			RECORDS				MATCH SCORES			
No	HOME		H	O	OPPONENT		SET 1	SET 2	SET 3	WINNER
1										
2										
3										
4										
5										
6										

DOUBLES			RECORDS				MATCH SCORES			
No	HOME		H	O	OPPONENT		SET 1	SET 2	SET 3	WINNER
1										
2										
3										

			TOTALS			

TENNIS SCORE SHEET

DATE	PLACE	TIME	WEATHER	COURT CONDITIONS	
HOME	LEAGUE	SEASON	OPPONENT	LEAGUE	SEASON

SINGLES

No	HOME	RECORDS H	RECORDS O	OPPONENT	MATCH SCORES SET 1	SET 2	SET 3	WINNER
1								
2								
3								
4								
5								
6								

DOUBLES

No	HOME	RECORDS H	RECORDS O	OPPONENT	MATCH SCORES SET 1	SET 2	SET 3	WINNER
1								
2								
3								

	TOTALS			

TENNIS SCORE SHEET

DATE	PLACE	TIME	WEATHER	COURT CONDITIONS	
HOME	LEAGUE	SEASON	OPPONENT	LEAGUE	SEASON

SINGLES		RECORDS			MATCH SCORES			
No	HOME	H	O	OPPONENT	SET 1	SET 2	SET 3	WINNER
1								
2								
3								
4								
5								
6								

DOUBLES		RECORDS			MATCH SCORES			
No	HOME	H	O	OPPONENT	SET 1	SET 2	SET 3	WINNER
1								
2								
3								

| | | | | | TOTALS | | | |

TENNIS SCORE SHEET

DATE	PLACE	TIME	WEATHER	COURT CONDITIONS	
HOME	LEAGUE	SEASON	OPPONENT	LEAGUE	SEASON

SINGLES

No	HOME	RECORDS H	RECORDS O	OPPONENT	SET 1	SET 2	SET 3	WINNER
					MATCH SCORES			
1								
2								
3								
4								
5								
6								

DOUBLES

No	HOME	RECORDS H	RECORDS O	OPPONENT	SET 1	SET 2	SET 3	WINNER
					MATCH SCORES			
1								
2								
3								

	TOTALS		

TENNIS SCORE SHEET

DATE	PLACE	TIME	WEATHER	COURT CONDITIONS	
HOME	LEAGUE	SEASON	OPPONENT	LEAGUE	SEASON

SINGLES

No	HOME	RECORDS H	RECORDS O	OPPONENT	SET 1	SET 2	SET 3	WINNER
					MATCH SCORES			
1								
2								
3								
4								
5								
6								

DOUBLES

No	HOME	RECORDS H	RECORDS O	OPPONENT	SET 1	SET 2	SET 3	WINNER
					MATCH SCORES			
1								
2								
3								

		TOTALS			

TENNIS SCORE SHEET

DATE	PLACE	TIME	WEATHER	COURT CONDITIONS	
HOME	LEAGUE	SEASON	OPPONENT	LEAGUE	SEASON

SINGLES

No	HOME	RECORDS		OPPONENT	MATCH SCORES			
		H	O		SET 1	SET 2	SET 3	WINNER
1								
2								
3								
4								
5								
6								

DOUBLES

No	HOME	RECORDS		OPPONENT	MATCH SCORES			
		H	O		SET 1	SET 2	SET 3	WINNER
1								
2								
3								

TOTALS			

TENNIS SCORE SHEET

DATE	PLACE	TIME	WEATHER	COURT CONDITIONS	
HOME	LEAGUE	SEASON	OPPONENT	LEAGUE	SEASON

SINGLES		RECORDS			MATCH SCORES			
No	HOME	H	O	OPPONENT	SET 1	SET 2	SET 3	WINNER
1								
2								
3								
4								
5								
6								

DOUBLES		RECORDS			MATCH SCORES			
No	HOME	H	O	OPPONENT	SET 1	SET 2	SET 3	WINNER
1								
2								
3								

TOTALS

TENNIS SCORE SHEET

DATE	PLACE	TIME	WEATHER	COURT CONDITIONS	
HOME	LEAGUE	SEASON	OPPONENT	LEAGUE	SEASON

SINGLES		RECORDS			MATCH SCORES			
No	HOME	H	O	OPPONENT	SET 1	SET 2	SET 3	WINNER
1								
2								
3								
4								
5								
6								

DOUBLES		RECORDS			MATCH SCORES			
No	HOME	H	O	OPPONENT	SET 1	SET 2	SET 3	WINNER
1								
2								
3								
				TOTALS				

TENNIS SCORE SHEET

DATE	PLACE	TIME	WEATHER	COURT CONDITIONS	
HOME	LEAGUE	SEASON	OPPONENT	LEAGUE	SEASON

SINGLES		RECORDS			MATCH SCORES			
No	HOME	H	O	OPPONENT	SET 1	SET 2	SET 3	WINNER
1								
2								
3								
4								
5								
6								

DOUBLES		RECORDS			MATCH SCORES			
No	HOME	H	O	OPPONENT	SET 1	SET 2	SET 3	WINNER
1								
2								
3								

TOTALS			

TENNIS SCORE SHEET

DATE	PLACE	TIME	WEATHER	COURT CONDITIONS	
HOME	LEAGUE	SEASON	OPPONENT	LEAGUE	SEASON

SINGLES

No	HOME	RECORDS		OPPONENT	MATCH SCORES			
		H	O		SET 1	SET 2	SET 3	WINNER
1								
2								
3								
4								
5								
6								

DOUBLES

No	HOME	RECORDS		OPPONENT	MATCH SCORES			
		H	O		SET 1	SET 2	SET 3	WINNER
1								
2								
3								

	TOTALS			

TENNIS SCORE SHEET

DATE	PLACE	TIME	WEATHER	COURT CONDITIONS	
HOME	LEAGUE	SEASON	OPPONENT	LEAGUE	SEASON

SINGLES		RECORDS			MATCH SCORES			
No	HOME	H	O	OPPONENT	SET 1	SET 2	SET 3	WINNER
1								
2								
3								
4								
5								
6								

DOUBLES		RECORDS			MATCH SCORES			
No	HOME	H	O	OPPONENT	SET 1	SET 2	SET 3	WINNER
1								
2								
3								

	TOTALS		

TENNIS SCORE SHEET

DATE	PLACE	TIME	WEATHER	COURT CONDITIONS	
HOME	LEAGUE	SEASON	OPPONENT	LEAGUE	SEASON

SINGLES

No	HOME	RECORDS H	RECORDS O	OPPONENT	SET 1	SET 2	SET 3	WINNER
1								
2								
3								
4								
5								
6								

MATCH SCORES (SET 1, SET 2, SET 3, WINNER)

DOUBLES

No	HOME	RECORDS H	RECORDS O	OPPONENT	SET 1	SET 2	SET 3	WINNER
1								
2								
3								

MATCH SCORES (SET 1, SET 2, SET 3, WINNER)

			TOTALS			

TENNIS SCORE SHEET

DATE	PLACE	TIME	WEATHER	COURT CONDITIONS	
HOME	LEAGUE	SEASON	OPPONENT	LEAGUE	SEASON

SINGLES			RECORDS		OPPONENT	MATCH SCORES			
No	HOME		H	O		SET 1	SET 2	SET 3	WINNER
1									
2									
3									
4									
5									
6									

DOUBLES			RECORDS		OPPONENT	MATCH SCORES			
No	HOME		H	O		SET 1	SET 2	SET 3	WINNER
1									
2									
3									
					TOTALS				

TENNIS SCORE SHEET

DATE	PLACE	TIME	WEATHER	COURT CONDITIONS	
HOME	LEAGUE	SEASON	OPPONENT	LEAGUE	SEASON

SINGLES

No	HOME	RECORDS H	RECORDS O	OPPONENT	SET 1	SET 2	SET 3	WINNER
					MATCH SCORES			
1								
2								
3								
4								
5								
6								

DOUBLES

No	HOME	RECORDS H	RECORDS O	OPPONENT	SET 1	SET 2	SET 3	WINNER
					MATCH SCORES			
1								
2								
3								

	TOTALS			

TENNIS SCORE SHEET

DATE	PLACE	TIME	WEATHER	COURT CONDITIONS	
HOME	LEAGUE	SEASON	OPPONENT	LEAGUE	SEASON

SINGLES

No	HOME	RECORDS H	RECORDS O	OPPONENT	SET 1	SET 2	SET 3	WINNER
					MATCH SCORES			
1								
2								
3								
4								
5								
6								

DOUBLES

No	HOME	RECORDS H	RECORDS O	OPPONENT	SET 1	SET 2	SET 3	WINNER
					MATCH SCORES			
1								
2								
3								

TOTALS

TENNIS SCORE SHEET

DATE	PLACE	TIME	WEATHER	COURT CONDITIONS	
HOME	LEAGUE	SEASON	OPPONENT	LEAGUE	SEASON

SINGLES		RECORDS			MATCH SCORES			
No	HOME	H	O	OPPONENT	SET 1	SET 2	SET 3	WINNER
1								
2								
3								
4								
5								
6								

DOUBLES		RECORDS			MATCH SCORES			
No	HOME	H	O	OPPONENT	SET 1	SET 2	SET 3	WINNER
1								
2								
3								

	TOTALS	

TENNIS SCORE SHEET

DATE	PLACE	TIME	WEATHER	COURT CONDITIONS	
HOME	LEAGUE	SEASON	OPPONENT	LEAGUE	SEASON

SINGLES		RECORDS			MATCH SCORES			
No	HOME	H	O	OPPONENT	SET 1	SET 2	SET 3	WINNER
1								
2								
3								
4								
5								
6								

DOUBLES		RECORDS			MATCH SCORES			
No	HOME	H	O	OPPONENT	SET 1	SET 2	SET 3	WINNER
1								
2								
3								

		TOTALS		

TENNIS SCORE SHEET

DATE	PLACE	TIME	WEATHER	COURT CONDITIONS	
HOME	LEAGUE	SEASON	OPPONENT	LEAGUE	SEASON

SINGLES

No	HOME	RECORDS H	RECORDS O	OPPONENT	MATCH SCORES SET 1	SET 2	SET 3	WINNER
1								
2								
3								
4								
5								
6								

DOUBLES

No	HOME	RECORDS H	RECORDS O	OPPONENT	MATCH SCORES SET 1	SET 2	SET 3	WINNER
1								
2								
3								

	TOTALS			

TENNIS SCORE SHEET

DATE	PLACE	TIME	WEATHER	COURT CONDITIONS	
HOME	LEAGUE	SEASON	OPPONENT	LEAGUE	SEASON

SINGLES			RECORDS			MATCH SCORES			
No	HOME		H	O	OPPONENT	SET 1	SET 2	SET 3	WINNER
1									
2									
3									
4									
5									
6									

DOUBLES			RECORDS			MATCH SCORES			
No	HOME		H	O	OPPONENT	SET 1	SET 2	SET 3	WINNER
1									
2									
3									

	TOTALS			

TENNIS SCORE SHEET

DATE	PLACE	TIME	WEATHER	COURT CONDITIONS	
HOME	LEAGUE	SEASON	OPPONENT	LEAGUE	SEASON

SINGLES

No	HOME	RECORDS H	RECORDS O	OPPONENT	SET 1	SET 2	SET 3	WINNER
1								
2								
3								
4								
5								
6								

RECORDS | **MATCH SCORES**

DOUBLES

No	HOME	RECORDS H	RECORDS O	OPPONENT	SET 1	SET 2	SET 3	WINNER
1								
2								
3								

RECORDS | **MATCH SCORES**

	TOTALS				

TENNIS SCORE SHEET

DATE	PLACE	TIME	WEATHER	COURT CONDITIONS	
HOME	LEAGUE	SEASON	OPPONENT	LEAGUE	SEASON

SINGLES		RECORDS			MATCH SCORES			
No	HOME	H	O	OPPONENT	SET 1	SET 2	SET 3	WINNER
1								
2								
3								
4								
5								
6								

DOUBLES		RECORDS			MATCH SCORES			
No	HOME	H	O	OPPONENT	SET 1	SET 2	SET 3	WINNER
1								
2								
3								

			TOTALS				

TENNIS SCORE SHEET

DATE	PLACE	TIME	WEATHER	COURT CONDITIONS	
HOME	LEAGUE	SEASON	OPPONENT	LEAGUE	SEASON

SINGLES

No	HOME	RECORDS H	RECORDS O	OPPONENT	SET 1	SET 2	SET 3	WINNER
1								
2								
3								
4								
5								
6								

RECORDS · **MATCH SCORES**

DOUBLES

No	HOME	RECORDS H	RECORDS O	OPPONENT	SET 1	SET 2	SET 3	WINNER
1								
2								
3								

RECORDS · **MATCH SCORES**

		TOTALS			

TENNIS SCORE SHEET

DATE	PLACE	TIME	WEATHER	COURT CONDITIONS	
HOME	LEAGUE	SEASON	OPPONENT	LEAGUE	SEASON

SINGLES

No	HOME	H	O	OPPONENT	SET 1	SET 2	SET 3	WINNER
1								
2								
3								
4								
5								
6								

DOUBLES

No	HOME	H	O	OPPONENT	SET 1	SET 2	SET 3	WINNER
1								
2								
3								

TOTALS

TENNIS SCORE SHEET

DATE	PLACE	TIME	WEATHER	COURT CONDITIONS	
HOME	LEAGUE	SEASON	OPPONENT	LEAGUE	SEASON

SINGLES

No	HOME	RECORDS H	RECORDS O	OPPONENT	SET 1	SET 2	SET 3	WINNER
1								
2								
3								
4								
5								
6								

MATCH SCORES

DOUBLES

No	HOME	RECORDS H	RECORDS O	OPPONENT	SET 1	SET 2	SET 3	WINNER
1								
2								
3								

MATCH SCORES

	TOTALS				

TENNIS SCORE SHEET

DATE	PLACE	TIME	WEATHER	COURT CONDITIONS	
HOME	LEAGUE	SEASON	OPPONENT	LEAGUE	SEASON

SINGLES

No	HOME	RECORDS H	RECORDS O	OPPONENT	SET 1	SET 2	SET 3	WINNER
1								
2								
3								
4								
5								
6								

MATCH SCORES

DOUBLES

No	HOME	RECORDS H	RECORDS O	OPPONENT	SET 1	SET 2	SET 3	WINNER
1								
2								
3								

MATCH SCORES

TOTALS				

TENNIS SCORE SHEET

DATE	PLACE	TIME	WEATHER	COURT CONDITIONS	
HOME	LEAGUE	SEASON	OPPONENT	LEAGUE	SEASON

SINGLES

No	HOME	RECORDS H	O	OPPONENT	SET 1	SET 2	SET 3	WINNER
1								
2								
3								
4								
5								
6								

RECORDS | **MATCH SCORES**

DOUBLES

No	HOME	RECORDS H	O	OPPONENT	SET 1	SET 2	SET 3	WINNER
1								
2								
3								

RECORDS | **MATCH SCORES**

	TOTALS			

TENNIS SCORE SHEET

DATE	PLACE	TIME	WEATHER	COURT CONDITIONS	
HOME	LEAGUE	SEASON	OPPONENT	LEAGUE	SEASON

SINGLES		RECORDS			MATCH SCORES			
No	HOME	H	O	OPPONENT	SET 1	SET 2	SET 3	WINNER
1								
2								
3								
4								
5								
6								

DOUBLES		RECORDS			MATCH SCORES			
No	HOME	H	O	OPPONENT	SET 1	SET 2	SET 3	WINNER
1								
2								
3								
				TOTALS				

TENNIS SCORE SHEET

DATE	PLACE	TIME	WEATHER	COURT CONDITIONS	
HOME	LEAGUE	SEASON	OPPONENT	LEAGUE	SEASON

SINGLES		RECORDS			MATCH SCORES			
No	HOME	H	O	OPPONENT	SET 1	SET 2	SET 3	WINNER
1								
2								
3								
4								
5								
6								

DOUBLES		RECORDS			MATCH SCORES			
No	HOME	H	O	OPPONENT	SET 1	SET 2	SET 3	WINNER
1								
2								
3								

				TOTALS			

TENNIS SCORE SHEET

DATE	PLACE	TIME	WEATHER	COURT CONDITIONS	
HOME	LEAGUE	SEASON	OPPONENT	LEAGUE	SEASON

SINGLES		RECORDS			MATCH SCORES			
No	HOME	H	O	OPPONENT	SET 1	SET 2	SET 3	WINNER
1								
2								
3								
4								
5								
6								

DOUBLES		RECORDS			MATCH SCORES			
No	HOME	H	O	OPPONENT	SET 1	SET 2	SET 3	WINNER
1								
2								
3								

TOTALS

TENNIS SCORE SHEET

DATE	PLACE	TIME	WEATHER	COURT CONDITIONS	
HOME	LEAGUE	SEASON	OPPONENT	LEAGUE	SEASON

SINGLES		RECORDS			MATCH SCORES			
No	HOME	H	O	OPPONENT	SET 1	SET 2	SET 3	WINNER
1								
2								
3								
4								
5								
6								

DOUBLES		RECORDS			MATCH SCORES			
No	HOME	H	O	OPPONENT	SET 1	SET 2	SET 3	WINNER
1								
2								
3								
			TOTALS					

TENNIS SCORE SHEET

DATE	PLACE	TIME	WEATHER	COURT CONDITIONS	
HOME	LEAGUE	SEASON	OPPONENT	LEAGUE	SEASON

SINGLES		RECORDS			MATCH SCORES			
No	HOME	H	O	OPPONENT	SET 1	SET 2	SET 3	WINNER
1								
2								
3								
4								
5								
6								

DOUBLES		RECORDS			MATCH SCORES			
No	HOME	H	O	OPPONENT	SET 1	SET 2	SET 3	WINNER
1								
2								
3								

	TOTALS			

TENNIS SCORE SHEET

DATE	PLACE	TIME	WEATHER	COURT CONDITIONS	
HOME	LEAGUE	SEASON	OPPONENT	LEAGUE	SEASON

SINGLES		RECORDS			MATCH SCORES			
No	HOME	H	O	OPPONENT	SET 1	SET 2	SET 3	WINNER
1								
2								
3								
4								
5								
6								

DOUBLES		RECORDS			MATCH SCORES			
No	HOME	H	O	OPPONENT	SET 1	SET 2	SET 3	WINNER
1								
2								
3								
			TOTALS					

TENNIS SCORE SHEET

DATE	PLACE	TIME	WEATHER	COURT CONDITIONS	
HOME	LEAGUE	SEASON	OPPONENT	LEAGUE	SEASON

SINGLES		RECORDS			MATCH SCORES			
No	HOME	H	O	OPPONENT	SET 1	SET 2	SET 3	WINNER
1								
2								
3								
4								
5								
6								

DOUBLES		RECORDS			MATCH SCORES			
No	HOME	H	O	OPPONENT	SET 1	SET 2	SET 3	WINNER
1								
2								
3								

TOTALS

TENNIS SCORE SHEET

DATE	PLACE	TIME	WEATHER	COURT CONDITIONS	
HOME	LEAGUE	SEASON	OPPONENT	LEAGUE	SEASON

SINGLES		RECORDS			MATCH SCORES			
No	HOME	H	O	OPPONENT	SET 1	SET 2	SET 3	WINNER
1								
2								
3								
4								
5								
6								

DOUBLES		RECORDS			MATCH SCORES			
No	HOME	H	O	OPPONENT	SET 1	SET 2	SET 3	WINNER
1								
2								
3								
				TOTALS				

TENNIS SCORE SHEET

DATE	PLACE	TIME	WEATHER	COURT CONDITIONS	
HOME	LEAGUE	SEASON	OPPONENT	LEAGUE	SEASON

SINGLES		RECORDS			MATCH SCORES			
No	HOME	H	O	OPPONENT	SET 1	SET 2	SET 3	WINNER
1								
2								
3								
4								
5								
6								

DOUBLES		RECORDS			MATCH SCORES			
No	HOME	H	O	OPPONENT	SET 1	SET 2	SET 3	WINNER
1								
2								
3								

	TOTALS			

TENNIS SCORE SHEET

DATE	PLACE	TIME	WEATHER	COURT CONDITIONS	
HOME	LEAGUE	SEASON	OPPONENT	LEAGUE	SEASON

SINGLES		RECORDS			MATCH SCORES			
No	HOME	H	O	OPPONENT	SET 1	SET 2	SET 3	WINNER
1								
2								
3								
4								
5								
6								

DOUBLES		RECORDS			MATCH SCORES			
No	HOME	H	O	OPPONENT	SET 1	SET 2	SET 3	WINNER
1								
2								
3								
				TOTALS				

TENNIS SCORE SHEET

DATE	PLACE	TIME	WEATHER	COURT CONDITIONS	
HOME	LEAGUE	SEASON	OPPONENT	LEAGUE	SEASON

SINGLES		RECORDS			MATCH SCORES			
No	HOME	H	O	OPPONENT	SET 1	SET 2	SET 3	WINNER
1								
2								
3								
4								
5								
6								

DOUBLES		RECORDS			MATCH SCORES			
No	HOME	H	O	OPPONENT	SET 1	SET 2	SET 3	WINNER
1								
2								
3								

TOTALS

TENNIS SCORE SHEET

DATE	PLACE	TIME	WEATHER	COURT CONDITIONS	
HOME	LEAGUE	SEASON	OPPONENT	LEAGUE	SEASON

SINGLES		RECORDS			MATCH SCORES			
No	HOME	H	O	OPPONENT	SET 1	SET 2	SET 3	WINNER
1								
2								
3								
4								
5								
6								

DOUBLES		RECORDS			MATCH SCORES			
No	HOME	H	O	OPPONENT	SET 1	SET 2	SET 3	WINNER
1								
2								
3								
			TOTALS					

TENNIS SCORE SHEET

DATE	PLACE	TIME	WEATHER	COURT CONDITIONS	
HOME	LEAGUE	SEASON	OPPONENT	LEAGUE	SEASON

SINGLES

No	HOME	RECORDS H	RECORDS O	OPPONENT	SET 1	SET 2	SET 3	WINNER
1								
2								
3								
4								
5								
6								

MATCH SCORES

DOUBLES

No	HOME	RECORDS H	RECORDS O	OPPONENT	SET 1	SET 2	SET 3	WINNER
1								
2								
3								

MATCH SCORES

TOTALS

TENNIS SCORE SHEET

DATE	PLACE	TIME	WEATHER	COURT CONDITIONS	
HOME	LEAGUE	SEASON	OPPONENT	LEAGUE	SEASON

SINGLES

No	HOME	RECORDS H	RECORDS O	OPPONENT	SET 1	SET 2	SET 3	WINNER
1								
2								
3								
4								
5								
6								

MATCH SCORES

DOUBLES

No	HOME	RECORDS H	RECORDS O	OPPONENT	SET 1	SET 2	SET 3	WINNER
1								
2								
3								

MATCH SCORES

	TOTALS				

TENNIS SCORE SHEET

DATE	PLACE	TIME	WEATHER	COURT CONDITIONS	
HOME	LEAGUE	SEASON	OPPONENT	LEAGUE	SEASON

SINGLES		RECORDS			MATCH SCORES			
No	HOME	H	O	OPPONENT	SET 1	SET 2	SET 3	WINNER
1								
2								
3								
4								
5								
6								

DOUBLES		RECORDS			MATCH SCORES			
No	HOME	H	O	OPPONENT	SET 1	SET 2	SET 3	WINNER
1								
2								
3								
		TOTALS						

TENNIS SCORE SHEET

DATE	PLACE	TIME	WEATHER	COURT CONDITIONS	
HOME	LEAGUE	SEASON	OPPONENT	LEAGUE	SEASON

SINGLES		RECORDS			MATCH SCORES			
No	HOME	H	O	OPPONENT	SET 1	SET 2	SET 3	WINNER
1								
2								
3								
4								
5								
6								

DOUBLES		RECORDS			MATCH SCORES			
No	HOME	H	O	OPPONENT	SET 1	SET 2	SET 3	WINNER
1								
2								
3								
				TOTALS				

TENNIS SCORE SHEET

DATE	PLACE	TIME	WEATHER	COURT CONDITIONS	
HOME	LEAGUE	SEASON	OPPONENT	LEAGUE	SEASON

SINGLES		RECORDS			MATCH SCORES			
No	HOME	H	O	OPPONENT	SET 1	SET 2	SET 3	WINNER
1								
2								
3								
4								
5								
6								

DOUBLES		RECORDS			MATCH SCORES			
No	HOME	H	O	OPPONENT	SET 1	SET 2	SET 3	WINNER
1								
2								
3								

		TOTALS			

TENNIS SCORE SHEET

DATE	PLACE	TIME	WEATHER	COURT CONDITIONS	
HOME	LEAGUE	SEASON	OPPONENT	LEAGUE	SEASON

SINGLES		RECORDS			MATCH SCORES			
No	HOME	H	O	OPPONENT	SET 1	SET 2	SET 3	WINNER
1								
2								
3								
4								
5								
6								

DOUBLES		RECORDS			MATCH SCORES			
No	HOME	H	O	OPPONENT	SET 1	SET 2	SET 3	WINNER
1								
2								
3								

		TOTALS			

TENNIS SCORE SHEET

DATE	PLACE	TIME	WEATHER	COURT CONDITIONS	
HOME	LEAGUE	SEASON	OPPONENT	LEAGUE	SEASON

SINGLES		RECORDS			MATCH SCORES			
No	HOME	H	O	OPPONENT	SET 1	SET 2	SET 3	WINNER
1								
2								
3								
4								
5								
6								

DOUBLES		RECORDS			MATCH SCORES			
No	HOME	H	O	OPPONENT	SET 1	SET 2	SET 3	WINNER
1								
2								
3								

TOTALS

TENNIS SCORE SHEET

DATE	PLACE	TIME	WEATHER	COURT CONDITIONS	
HOME	LEAGUE	SEASON	OPPONENT	LEAGUE	SEASON

SINGLES		RECORDS				MATCH SCORES			
No	HOME	H	O	OPPONENT		SET 1	SET 2	SET 3	WINNER
1									
2									
3									
4									
5									
6									

DOUBLES		RECORDS				MATCH SCORES			
No	HOME	H	O	OPPONENT		SET 1	SET 2	SET 3	WINNER
1									
2									
3									

		TOTALS			

TENNIS SCORE SHEET

DATE	PLACE	TIME	WEATHER	COURT CONDITIONS	
HOME	LEAGUE	SEASON	OPPONENT	LEAGUE	SEASON

SINGLES		RECORDS			MATCH SCORES			
No	HOME	H	O	OPPONENT	SET 1	SET 2	SET 3	WINNER
1								
2								
3								
4								
5								
6								

DOUBLES		RECORDS			MATCH SCORES			
No	HOME	H	O	OPPONENT	SET 1	SET 2	SET 3	WINNER
1								
2								
3								

					TOTALS		

TENNIS SCORE SHEET

DATE	PLACE	TIME	WEATHER	COURT CONDITIONS	
HOME	LEAGUE	SEASON	OPPONENT	LEAGUE	SEASON

SINGLES		RECORDS			MATCH SCORES			
No	HOME	H	O	OPPONENT	SET 1	SET 2	SET 3	WINNER
1								
2								
3								
4								
5								
6								

DOUBLES		RECORDS			MATCH SCORES			
No	HOME	H	O	OPPONENT	SET 1	SET 2	SET 3	WINNER
1								
2								
3								

		TOTALS			

TENNIS SCORE SHEET

DATE	PLACE	TIME	WEATHER	COURT CONDITIONS	
HOME	LEAGUE	SEASON	OPPONENT	LEAGUE	SEASON

	SINGLES	RECORDS			MATCH SCORES			
No	HOME	H	O	OPPONENT	SET 1	SET 2	SET 3	WINNER
1								
2								
3								
4								
5								
6								

	DOUBLES	RECORDS			MATCH SCORES			
No	HOME	H	O	OPPONENT	SET 1	SET 2	SET 3	WINNER
1								
2								
3								

			TOTALS			

TENNIS SCORE SHEET

DATE	PLACE	TIME	WEATHER	COURT CONDITIONS	
HOME	LEAGUE	SEASON	OPPONENT	LEAGUE	SEASON

SINGLES

No	HOME	RECORDS H	RECORDS O	OPPONENT	SET 1	SET 2	SET 3	WINNER
1								
2								
3								
4								
5								
6								

RECORDS — MATCH SCORES

DOUBLES

No	HOME	RECORDS H	RECORDS O	OPPONENT	SET 1	SET 2	SET 3	WINNER
1								
2								
3								

RECORDS — MATCH SCORES

	TOTALS		

TENNIS SCORE SHEET

DATE	PLACE	TIME	WEATHER	COURT CONDITIONS	
HOME	LEAGUE	SEASON	OPPONENT	LEAGUE	SEASON

SINGLES		RECORDS			MATCH SCORES			
No	HOME	H	O	OPPONENT	SET 1	SET 2	SET 3	WINNER
1								
2								
3								
4								
5								
6								

DOUBLES		RECORDS			MATCH SCORES			
No	HOME	H	O	OPPONENT	SET 1	SET 2	SET 3	WINNER
1								
2								
3								

TOTALS	

TENNIS SCORE SHEET

DATE	PLACE	TIME	WEATHER	COURT CONDITIONS	
HOME	LEAGUE	SEASON	OPPONENT	LEAGUE	SEASON

SINGLES

No	HOME	RECORDS H	RECORDS O	OPPONENT	SET 1	SET 2	SET 3	WINNER
1								
2								
3								
4								
5								
6								

DOUBLES

No	HOME	RECORDS H	RECORDS O	OPPONENT	SET 1	SET 2	SET 3	WINNER
1								
2								
3								

| | | | | TOTALS | | | | |

TENNIS SCORE SHEET

DATE	PLACE	TIME	WEATHER	COURT CONDITIONS	
HOME	LEAGUE	SEASON	OPPONENT	LEAGUE	SEASON

SINGLES		RECORDS			MATCH SCORES			
No	HOME	H	O	OPPONENT	SET 1	SET 2	SET 3	WINNER
1								
2								
3								
4								
5								
6								

DOUBLES		RECORDS			MATCH SCORES			
No	HOME	H	O	OPPONENT	SET 1	SET 2	SET 3	WINNER
1								
2								
3								

	TOTALS		

TENNIS SCORE SHEET

DATE	PLACE	TIME	WEATHER	COURT CONDITIONS	
HOME	LEAGUE	SEASON	OPPONENT	LEAGUE	SEASON

SINGLES		RECORDS			MATCH SCORES			
No	HOME	H	O	OPPONENT	SET 1	SET 2	SET 3	WINNER
1								
2								
3								
4								
5								
6								

DOUBLES		RECORDS			MATCH SCORES			
No	HOME	H	O	OPPONENT	SET 1	SET 2	SET 3	WINNER
1								
2								
3								

TOTALS

TENNIS SCORE SHEET

DATE	PLACE	TIME	WEATHER	COURT CONDITIONS	
HOME	LEAGUE	SEASON	OPPONENT	LEAGUE	SEASON

SINGLES		RECORDS			MATCH SCORES			
No	HOME	H	O	OPPONENT	SET 1	SET 2	SET 3	WINNER
1								
2								
3								
4								
5								
6								

DOUBLES		RECORDS			MATCH SCORES			
No	HOME	H	O	OPPONENT	SET 1	SET 2	SET 3	WINNER
1								
2								
3								
			TOTALS					

TENNIS SCORE SHEET

DATE	PLACE	TIME	WEATHER	COURT CONDITIONS	
HOME	LEAGUE	SEASON	OPPONENT	LEAGUE	SEASON

SINGLES		RECORDS			MATCH SCORES			
No	HOME	H	O	OPPONENT	SET 1	SET 2	SET 3	WINNER
1								
2								
3								
4								
5								
6								

DOUBLES		RECORDS			MATCH SCORES			
No	HOME	H	O	OPPONENT	SET 1	SET 2	SET 3	WINNER
1								
2								
3								

	TOTALS			

TENNIS SCORE SHEET

DATE	PLACE	TIME	WEATHER	COURT CONDITIONS	
HOME	LEAGUE	SEASON	OPPONENT	LEAGUE	SEASON

SINGLES		RECORDS			MATCH SCORES			
No	HOME	H	O	OPPONENT	SET 1	SET 2	SET 3	WINNER
1								
2								
3								
4								
5								
6								

DOUBLES		RECORDS			MATCH SCORES			
No	HOME	H	O	OPPONENT	SET 1	SET 2	SET 3	WINNER
1								
2								
3								
				TOTALS				

TENNIS SCORE SHEET

DATE	PLACE	TIME	WEATHER	COURT CONDITIONS	
HOME	LEAGUE	SEASON	OPPONENT	LEAGUE	SEASON

SINGLES		RECORDS			MATCH SCORES			
No	HOME	H	O	OPPONENT	SET 1	SET 2	SET 3	WINNER
1								
2								
3								
4								
5								
6								

DOUBLES		RECORDS			MATCH SCORES			
No	HOME	H	O	OPPONENT	SET 1	SET 2	SET 3	WINNER
1								
2								
3								
				TOTALS				

TENNIS SCORE SHEET

DATE	PLACE	TIME	WEATHER	COURT CONDITIONS	
HOME	LEAGUE	SEASON	OPPONENT	LEAGUE	SEASON

SINGLES

No	HOME	H	O	OPPONENT	SET 1	SET 2	SET 3	WINNER
		RECORDS			**MATCH SCORES**			
1								
2								
3								
4								
5								
6								

DOUBLES

No	HOME	H	O	OPPONENT	SET 1	SET 2	SET 3	WINNER
		RECORDS			**MATCH SCORES**			
1								
2								
3								
			TOTALS					

TENNIS SCORE SHEET

DATE	PLACE	TIME	WEATHER	COURT CONDITIONS	
HOME	LEAGUE	SEASON	OPPONENT	LEAGUE	SEASON

SINGLES		RECORDS			MATCH SCORES			
No	HOME	H	O	OPPONENT	SET 1	SET 2	SET 3	WINNER
1								
2								
3								
4								
5								
6								

DOUBLES		RECORDS			MATCH SCORES			
No	HOME	H	O	OPPONENT	SET 1	SET 2	SET 3	WINNER
1								
2								
3								

	TOTALS			

TENNIS SCORE SHEET

DATE	PLACE	TIME	WEATHER	COURT CONDITIONS	
HOME	LEAGUE	SEASON	OPPONENT	LEAGUE	SEASON

SINGLES		RECORDS			MATCH SCORES			
No	HOME	H	O	OPPONENT	SET 1	SET 2	SET 3	WINNER
1								
2								
3								
4								
5								
6								

DOUBLES		RECORDS			MATCH SCORES			
No	HOME	H	O	OPPONENT	SET 1	SET 2	SET 3	WINNER
1								
2								
3								
		TOTALS						

TENNIS SCORE SHEET

DATE	PLACE	TIME	WEATHER	COURT CONDITIONS	
HOME	LEAGUE	SEASON	OPPONENT	LEAGUE	SEASON

SINGLES		RECORDS			MATCH SCORES			
No	HOME	H	O	OPPONENT	SET 1	SET 2	SET 3	WINNER
1								
2								
3								
4								
5								
6								

DOUBLES		RECORDS			MATCH SCORES			
No	HOME	H	O	OPPONENT	SET 1	SET 2	SET 3	WINNER
1								
2								
3								

	TOTALS			

TENNIS SCORE SHEET

DATE	PLACE	TIME	WEATHER	COURT CONDITIONS	
HOME	LEAGUE	SEASON	OPPONENT	LEAGUE	SEASON

SINGLES		RECORDS			MATCH SCORES			
No	HOME	H	O	OPPONENT	SET 1	SET 2	SET 3	WINNER
1								
2								
3								
4								
5								
6								

DOUBLES		RECORDS			MATCH SCORES			
No	HOME	H	O	OPPONENT	SET 1	SET 2	SET 3	WINNER
1								
2								
3								
				TOTALS				

TENNIS SCORE SHEET

DATE	PLACE	TIME	WEATHER	COURT CONDITIONS	
HOME	LEAGUE	SEASON	OPPONENT	LEAGUE	SEASON

SINGLES		RECORDS			MATCH SCORES			
No	HOME	H	O	OPPONENT	SET 1	SET 2	SET 3	WINNER
1								
2								
3								
4								
5								
6								

DOUBLES		RECORDS			MATCH SCORES			
No	HOME	H	O	OPPONENT	SET 1	SET 2	SET 3	WINNER
1								
2								
3								

	TOTALS			

TENNIS SCORE SHEET

DATE	PLACE	TIME	WEATHER	COURT CONDITIONS	
HOME	LEAGUE	SEASON	OPPONENT	LEAGUE	SEASON

SINGLES		RECORDS			MATCH SCORES			
No	HOME	H	O	OPPONENT	SET 1	SET 2	SET 3	WINNER
1								
2								
3								
4								
5								
6								

DOUBLES		RECORDS			MATCH SCORES			
No	HOME	H	O	OPPONENT	SET 1	SET 2	SET 3	WINNER
1								
2								
3								
			TOTALS					

TENNIS SCORE SHEET

DATE	PLACE	TIME	WEATHER	COURT CONDITIONS	
HOME	LEAGUE	SEASON	OPPONENT	LEAGUE	SEASON

SINGLES		RECORDS			MATCH SCORES			
No	HOME	H	O	OPPONENT	SET 1	SET 2	SET 3	WINNER
1								
2								
3								
4								
5								
6								

DOUBLES		RECORDS			MATCH SCORES			
No	HOME	H	O	OPPONENT	SET 1	SET 2	SET 3	WINNER
1								
2								
3								

	TOTALS	

TENNIS SCORE SHEET

DATE	PLACE	TIME	WEATHER	COURT CONDITIONS	
HOME	*LEAGUE*	*SEASON*	*OPPONENT*	*LEAGUE*	*SEASON*

	SINGLES	RECORDS			MATCH SCORES			
No	HOME	H	O	OPPONENT	SET 1	SET 2	SET 3	WINNER
1								
2								
3								
4								
5								
6								

	DOUBLES	RECORDS			MATCH SCORES			
No	HOME	H	O	OPPONENT	SET 1	SET 2	SET 3	WINNER
1								
2								
3								

	TOTALS			

TENNIS SCORE SHEET

DATE	PLACE	TIME	WEATHER	COURT CONDITIONS	
HOME	LEAGUE	SEASON	OPPONENT	LEAGUE	SEASON

SINGLES

No	HOME	RECORDS H	RECORDS O	OPPONENT	SET 1	SET 2	SET 3	WINNER
1								
2								
3								
4								
5								
6								

RECORDS — H / O
MATCH SCORES — SET 1 | SET 2 | SET 3 | WINNER

DOUBLES

No	HOME	RECORDS H	RECORDS O	OPPONENT	SET 1	SET 2	SET 3	WINNER
1								
2								
3								

RECORDS — H / O
MATCH SCORES — SET 1 | SET 2 | SET 3 | WINNER

TOTALS

TENNIS SCORE SHEET

DATE	PLACE	TIME	WEATHER	COURT CONDITIONS	
HOME	LEAGUE	SEASON	OPPONENT	LEAGUE	SEASON

SINGLES		RECORDS			MATCH SCORES			
No	HOME	H	O	OPPONENT	SET 1	SET 2	SET 3	WINNER
1								
2								
3								
4								
5								
6								

DOUBLES		RECORDS			MATCH SCORES			
No	HOME	H	O	OPPONENT	SET 1	SET 2	SET 3	WINNER
1								
2								
3								

				TOTALS			

TENNIS SCORE SHEET

DATE	PLACE	TIME	WEATHER	COURT CONDITIONS	
HOME	LEAGUE	SEASON	OPPONENT	LEAGUE	SEASON

SINGLES

No	HOME	RECORDS H	RECORDS O	OPPONENT	SET 1	SET 2	SET 3	WINNER
1								
2								
3								
4								
5								
6								

MATCH SCORES

DOUBLES

No	HOME	RECORDS H	RECORDS O	OPPONENT	SET 1	SET 2	SET 3	WINNER
1								
2								
3								

MATCH SCORES

TOTALS

TENNIS SCORE SHEET

DATE	PLACE	TIME	WEATHER	COURT CONDITIONS	
HOME	LEAGUE	SEASON	OPPONENT	LEAGUE	SEASON

SINGLES		RECORDS			MATCH SCORES			
No	HOME	H	O	OPPONENT	SET 1	SET 2	SET 3	WINNER
1								
2								
3								
4								
5								
6								

DOUBLES		RECORDS			MATCH SCORES			
No	HOME	H	O	OPPONENT	SET 1	SET 2	SET 3	WINNER
1								
2								
3								

		TOTALS			

Made in the USA
San Bernardino, CA
04 February 2019